My Best Book of Ancient Greece

Belinda Weber

Contents

KINGFISHER

Kingfisher Publications Plc
New Penderel House
283–288 High Holborn
London WC1V 7HZ

Author: Belinda Weber
Publishing manager: Melissa Fairley
Art director: Mike Davis
Consultant: Dr Thorsten Opper,
The British Museum

Main illustrations by Chris Molan

First published by Kingfisher
Publications Plc 2005

10 9 8 7 6 5 4 3 2 1

1TR/0305/WKT/SGCH(SGCH)/128KMA/C

A CIP catalogue record for this book
is available from the British Library.

ISBN-13: 978 0 7534 1103 2
ISBN-10: 0 7534 1103 2

Printed in China

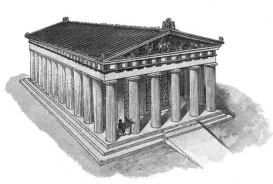

The early Greeks

The first people to live in Greece – almost 40,000 years ago – were Stone Age hunter-gatherers. They moved from place to place in search of food. As people learned to farm the land, they grew crops and stayed in the same place. Small groups of people could live together happily, without having to worry about finding food. Early civilizations developed on the Cyclades islands in the Aegean Sea. The Minoans settled on the island of Crete.

The Palace of Knossos

The Minoans decorated the walls of this palace in Crete with beautiful paintings. They often painted the creatures they could see from the island, such as dolphins and fish.

Early writing

Many Minoans could read and write. They turned the picture writing of ancient Egypt into a style of handwriting, which was called Linear A.

A

Living the high life

Minoans were farmers who grew crops such as wheat, barley, olives and grapes. They also raised sheep, goats and cattle for meat and milk. They built huge palaces, the finest of which was at Knossos.

4

Aegean
Sea

Greece

Cyclades
islands

Early Greek
settlements

Crete

The Mycenaeans

At about the same time as the Minoans were living on Crete, another civilization developed on the mainland. The Mycenaeans were warriors and they were ruled by kings. They also traded farm produce and pottery for gold and ivory. Mycenaean craftsmen were very skilful and made many beautiful objects including fine pottery and gold ornaments.

Funerary mask

Painting of a hunt

Fine craftsmanship

With a settled society, not everyone had to farm the land in order to produce enough food to eat. Some people developed other skills. Craftsmen used local clay to make decorated plates and goblets. They then traded these for gold from which to make fine funerary masks. These masks were used in royal burials.

Strong walls

The Mycenaeans built their city on top of a hill, so they could see any attackers as they approached. The city had strong walls, made from huge blocks of stone, and the gate was decorated with two lions. No one knows why, but the city was abandoned or destroyed by around 1100BCE.

The tale of Troy

 **When Mycenae's major cities were destroyed, Greece entered the Dark Age.** People did not learn to read, but listened to poets telling the great stories from the past. One poet, Homer, tells of how Helen, the wife of the king of Sparta, was kidnapped and taken to Troy. It explains how the Greeks tricked the Trojans into letting them into their city.

The Trojan Horse

The Greeks made a huge wooden horse which they left outside Troy's city walls. The Trojans were curious and dragged it inside. That night, soldiers hidden inside the horse, crept out and opened the city gates, letting the Greek army in to destroy the city.

Heinrich Schliemann studied the ruins of Troy.

Finding out

German archaeologist Heinrich Schliemann discovered that Troy was on the Mediterranean coast of modern-day Turkey. His research found not just one city there, but many, all built on top of each other.

Settling new lands

No one knows exactly what happened during the Dark Ages. We think people no longer learned to read or write, and that is why they did not keep written records. As populations grew, there was not enough food for everyone. Trading posts were set up and Greeks started to settle new lands. They moved around the Mediterranean coasts, to Italy, Sicily, Africa, France and Spain. With easy access to the sea, the new settlements began to trade wine, olive oil and honey for grain and timber.

Settlers arriving at a new colony

Trade

The Greeks were successful farmers and traded their surplus crops for other items. Greek craftsmen used the new materials to make bangles and pottery.

New colonies

Many of the new colonies were set up around the Mediterranean and Black Sea coasts. These places had good natural harbours and plentiful farming land.

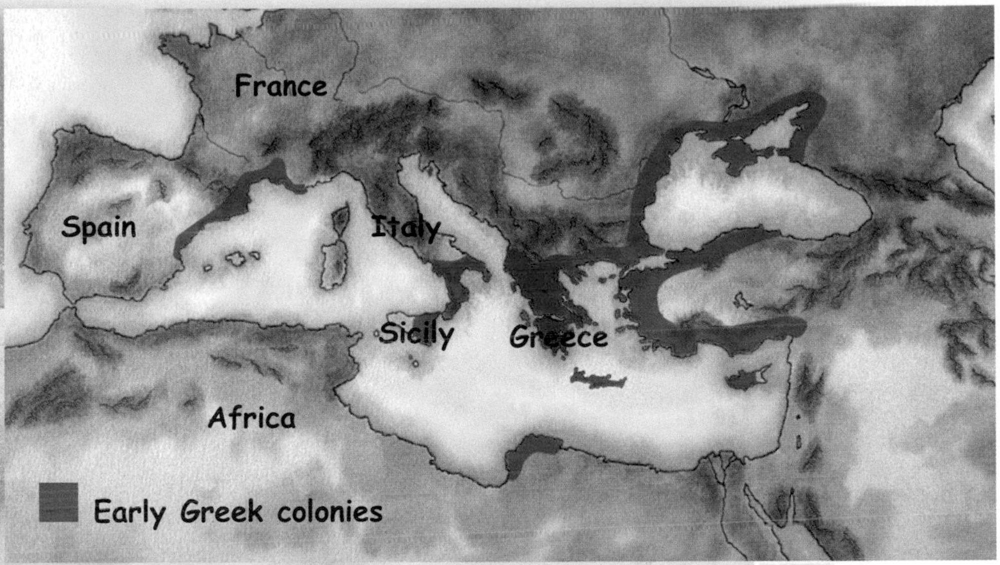

France

Spain

Italy

Sicily   Greece

Africa

■ Early Greek colonies

Building new homes

The new colonies built temples and houses for the new community.

The rise of Athens

The Greeks who stayed behind formed 'city-states', which were made up of the city and the surrounding countryside. The largest was Athens, which was rich and powerful as it had its own silver mines and a port. After the expulsion of the last tyrannical ruler, Athens was run by citizens – men who were born in the city and could vote to say how their city was run. It was the first democracy, where citizens made decisions.

Athena

Athens was named after Athena, the goddess of wisdom and warfare. The Greeks built the Parthenon, which contained a huge statue, because they believed Athena protected the city.

Having a say

City-states had their own governments and ways of doing things. Meetings were held about 40 times a year and all citizens could vote.

Greek citizens had the chance to question other people's political views during debates.

People inside the Parthenon

Sparta

Sparta was another important city-state. It was ruled by two kings and had a council which made all the decisions – they were very strict and demanded obedience from their people. All Spartans, men and women alike, had to be physically fit and trained in warfare. Spartan soldiers were the strongest in Greece.

Training hard

Life was tough in Sparta. Only the fittest babies were allowed to live – officials decided which new-borns would survive. Boys left home aged seven to be brought up with other boys. They trained hard and became soldiers.

14

The man behind the idea

Lycurgus was the ancient Greek statesman who set up the military city-state of Sparta. Lycurgus showed that military training and physical fitness gave the Spartans an advantage when fighting other city-states.

The oracle at Delphi was said to have foretold the laws of Sparta. Her priest read the laws to Lycurgus.

Girl power

Spartan girls were also expected to be fit so that they could produce healthy babies. They were encouraged to compete in athletics.

15

Great ideas

Ancient Greece was the home of many great ideas. Regular meetings were held at which any citizen was allowed to speak. A well-presented argument could change the way people voted, which meant education was also important. Boys were taught to read, write and make speeches.

The Greeks brought offerings to the god Asclepius in the hope he would heal them.

Understanding maths

Archimedes, a great mathematician, was in his bath when he solved a mathematical problem. He shouted out 'eureka', which means 'I've got it'.

Father of medicine

The ancient Greeks understood how the body works and were able to treat many ailments. They also prayed to Asclepius, the god of medicine. The Greeks offered pictures or carvings of their wounded limbs in the hope that Asclepius would cure them, and many believed that sleeping in his temples would improve their health.

Political life

Citizens' meetings were held outside the
city walls, on a hill called the Pnyx which
was near the Acropolis. An Assembly
was the most important type of meeting.
Voters decided on political issues here.

Daily life

In ancient Greece, most married couples lived in households made up of their elderly parents, children and slaves.

Men born in the city-state were called citizens and had the right to vote. Women, foreigners and slaves did not have this right, and had to follow the decisions made by the man of their household. Very few women held powerful positions in society.

Storeroom

Greek streets were often smelly and dirty, with open drains. Most houses faced away from the street.

Toys and games

Greek children did not have long to enjoy their childhood. By the time they were 15 years old, many boys were training for the army, while most girls were married. There were no schools, but boys from wealthy families were taught by private tutors. However, Greek children still found time for toys, including dolls and toy horses.

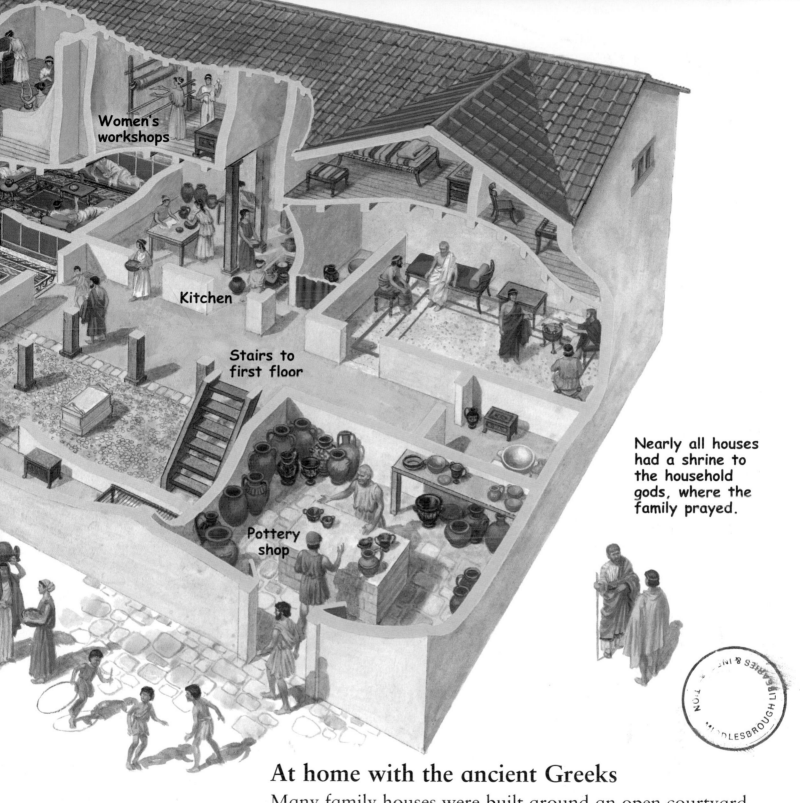

Women's workshops

Kitchen

Stairs to first floor

Pottery shop

Nearly all houses had a shrine to the household gods, where the family prayed.

At home with the ancient Greeks

Many family houses were built around an open courtyard, with the rooms opening on to it. This house is also a potter's workshop and shop. The family lived at the back, with their bedrooms and the women's workshops upstairs. Any slaves would also have lived upstairs.

Festivals and games

The Greeks always made time for theatre, music and dancing. Physical fitness was greatly prized and the Olympic Games were held in honour of the god Zeus. Like other sporting competitions, the Olympic Games were open to all Greek city-states and there was fierce rivalry. Champions were crowned with olive leaves.

Good sports

If city-states were at war with each other when the Olympic Games were held, a truce was called so that everyone could take part. Winning athletes were treated as heroes.

Many of the sports in the Olympic Games are still practised today. Throwing the javelin is one of them.

20

The theatre

The Greeks loved going to the theatre. All the parts were played by men, who wore masks or brightly coloured clothes to show their character.

3
Winning the Olympics

Winners were rewarded with crowns of olive leaves and had ribbons tied to their arms. They were given free food for life in their home city-state.

2
Racing apart

Girls were not allowed to take part in the same competitions as the boys – they had their own races.

Armies and war

Only in Sparta was there a full-time, fully trained army. In other city-states all citizens were part-time soldiers who were expected to drop everything and help fight in times of war. Most wars only lasted a few weeks, and survivors were soon back home.

Eyes and faces were sometimes painted on to the ships to make them look more frightening.

Foot soldiers

Greek foot soldiers were called hoplites and were a very important part of the army. Many Greek battles were fought with lines of hoplites marching up to the enemy and hacking their way through.

Fighting at sea

Many Greek battles were fought at sea. Special warships, called triremes, were used. Teams of 170 oarsmen rowed the ships, powering them along at great speed. The ships had a huge battering ram at the front, to crash into enemy ships and cause the maximum damage.

Fighting on horses

Soldiers had to buy their own armour and horses, so only the wealthy could afford to ride. They formed the cavalry, and could charge into enemy lines, making gaps for the hoplites.

Gods and goddesses

The ancient Greeks believed that gods and goddesses controlled every aspect of nature and had power over their lives. Each city or town had a guardian god or goddess to look after them, and temples were built in their honour. Ceremonies were also held to ask for their protection.

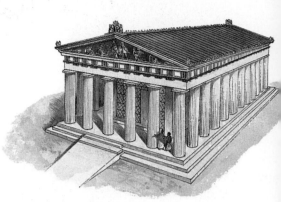

Temples
Ornate temples were built to please the gods. People prayed to the gods to help them with their lives.

Generous Greeks
The Greeks offered sacrifices to their gods. These could be an animal, usually a sheep, or wine or oil. Each offering showed that the Greeks were generous to the gods.

Gods at war
Even the gods fought wars and battles. In one myth, Zeus led the Olympian gods against the Titans – the Titan leader, Kronos, was Zeus' father.

Myths and legends

The ancient Greeks thought their gods lived as a huge family beyond the clouds over Mount Olympus. Their gods looked like humans and had many of the same qualities and faults – they even argued and fell out with each other. The Greeks celebrated their gods with stories and legends telling of great acts of courage and bravery. These stories helped them to understand the world in which they lived.

Flying horses

Pegasus was a winged horse that carried the hero Bellerophon into battle. But when he tried to ride into heaven, the gods got angry. Pegasus was stung by an insect and threw Bellerophon off his back.

One-eyed monsters

Cyclops was a storm god who made thunderbolts for Zeus. Legend tells how the hero Odysseus defeated Cyclops in one of his many adventures.

Into the Labyrinth

When Theseus set out to kill the minotaur that lived in a maze called the Labyrinth, he unwound a ball of wool as he walked. After killing the monster, he found his way back safely, following the wool.

How do we know?

Wealthy Europeans started collecting statues and pottery from ancient Greece in the 18th century CE.

Archaeologists studied buildings to learn more about the history of the places. They also found pottery and works of art which helped them understand how people lived.

Temple carvings

Many temple walls were decorated with carvings. They tell us how important the gods were to the people and how they worshipped.

Written records

Many inscriptions were carved in stone. They help us to understand more about daily life for the ancient Greeks.

Digging up history

At an excavation, great care is taken not to damage any of the remains. The soil is sieved to make sure nothing is missed, and every find is checked carefully.

Greece today

Many of the temples and buildings mentioned in this book can still be seen today. Greek cities, such as Athens, bustle with life and are popular places for tourists to visit. The mixture of ancient and new gives a sense of history, while allowing people to enjoy a modern lifestyle.

The Parthenon

Originally built as a temple, the Parthenon remains an inspiring place to visit. It is made of stone and marble, and has beautiful detailed carvings in the panels.

Tourists visiting the Parthenon

Glossary

ailment A minor illness or disease.

ceremony A ritual, or formal act, performed to mark a special occasion.

city-state A Greek city and surroundings that had its own government.

colonies New settlements set up away from the mainland, but often paid for by the Greeks.

courtyard An outside area within the walls of the house, open to the sky.

craftsmanship Skill at making works of art.

Dark Age A time period about which little is known.

democracy A system of government in which citizens can vote on issues. Citizens usually elect representatives.

funerary masks Decorative masks that are placed over the faces of dead people before burial. They usually look like the person.

guardian Someone who looks after someone else.

minotaur A mythical creature that was half-man, half-bull.

oracle A spirit who could foretell the future or give wise advice – often speaking through priestesses.

ornate Beautifully decorated.

shrine An altar or place at which to worship a god.

survivors Those who remain alive or undamaged in spite of an event.

thunderbolts Powerful blasts of thunder that were used by the gods.

trading posts Places where surplus goods and foods could be sold or swapped for other goods.

truce An agreement to stop fighting.

tyrannical Describes an absolute ruler, but one who has taken power by force.

Index